# STERLING 403

## David McAleavey

STERLING 403

# STERLING 403

## David McAleavey

an Ithaca House book

Ithaca

Some of these poems appear in *Chicago Review*, *Cloud Marauder*, *Epoch*, *Intro 4*, *Occident*, *Rainy Day*, and *The Stone*.

The section *he speaks* on pp. 62 & 63 is quoted from the second of Rene Descartes' *Meditations on First Philosophy*.

ITHACA HOUSE, 314 FOREST HOME DRIVE
ITHACA, NEW YORK 14850

To David Sachs

# CONTENTS

## HEIRESS

as a child you
coaxed wild rabbits
to eat from your hand but
didn't tell us you knew they were pets
of the motel manager's daughter

— to please us you were

sporting
with the rabbits

— the earliest photo, we thought
"candid"

nothing for you was hidden, even
the camera's intervention —

now your arousal
is ruse.

you use drugs for the purpose/
you write poems,
give "poetry" a greek
twang,
quarrel easily as if
you want to confuse us —

                                  still,
                              you see us all
                  as clockworks
                      without cases;
                  you wear sunglasses!

        what can I say
     – you wear sunglasses,
     your privilege –
     as ice you melt through us.

RECORD

We slipped out of the focus
of the old man's kodak
and entered the formal garden.
The high hedge of the maze
kept the wind from our clothes.
There was maybe a center
where the aisles led? some altar
to Pan, some graceless nude....
We walked in step, pressing
the gravel to the mud
from yesterday's rain.
The sky was normal for that season
and place. The sense of the garden
was lost in further conjectures.
Back on the street the old man
was getting on the bus downtown:
his camera, neatly cased, hung
at his side.

## CONSTRUCTION

The girl playing with the plastic cup,
her head barely table high,
saw me. I saw John Deere
Loader 150 Series B, yellow
in the night, surrounded,
Danger construction,
excavation,    Warning:
Olin Safety Flares, their
magenta eyes. Summer
is upon us though we huddle
through the wind, Mary, Mary,
this is the way he came, hungry
for happiness, all his years
in subtle grins, secret wars —
"You must be a cool man" —
an admiring Irish voice. Or
did they find him out, cruel
and preservative.... The moon
and news is not assuring.
The torn cup was thrown
into a barrel by the busboy
and waits for burning.
Gravity moves downward,
where we become, is it not wise,
is it not wise, the ground, danger.

## TABLE

the solitaire we play & mountains
we would like to be living in;
our mothball clothes
unsuited to this climate
and the times:

           all the versions
of solitaire we play,
the uses we put
& aims we abandon
ourselves to.

*aspens, birch*

we move away —
if that is too hard we move
again. we move again
& then we do not move at all.

under rotting varnish
the cedar smells good
tho lifetimes
fool at the surface.

## DECLARATION

Also, in love, I was cheated
and cheated several times —
one moon for the beautiful faces,
one sun engaging the gears
of the world. Every day, les oiseaux,
the new dawn, with no duels to settle it,
"Concrete, concrete, you could have filled
Lake Boden with it all." Swans
in the castle waters, pelicans
fishing off the Keys, coots
in Wisconsin. The beak, the prow,
friends, let me lecture;
and then let me go.

## DECORATOR

the south wall, in the
corner by the window,

you cover with food. the
west wall with schedules &

calendars. drawings of
interiors cover the north

while you fill the east
wall with lithographs

& photos of yourself,
which you hardly

recognize. & now you pull
the chain & the overhead

lights up. the room is
there, finished. you turn the

light off. it is night. are
you there, finally

finished, you ask, is
the room, is the middle

of the room, are you the
middle, still, there, or out.

## SCYTHE

The sun moves. The scythe I wielded then
moved and moved on the weeds. Silent
contortions, your face when it hit.
Everyone avoided their intentions
when they saw you, and ran. I stayed
all July, for the celebrations; heat
rose over the road. In the grass
ticks waited. The arm with the black
glove reached and pinched the cigarette.
You have not heard this story before.
And reached the cigarette into the sky.

The noise our frames make, falling,
or our hair, burning. They find
several states of nudity. I appeal
to your suggestion concerning madness:
my body is unfamiliar every time
and yours I cannot follow. Schedules
for August failed to mention the danger.
Beyond the window of this hotel we climb
slantwise to the wind. There is a pause.
We join and shower. "If you are well
I am well." Someone else holds the scythe.

## SAILBOAT METAPHOR # 4

salience.    a quality
as the instance, a puddle
a boat
journey under wind
 reeling from
all further dictations
       which relics
fill & fill
settles.
         still no memory
wrenches.    the only use
I ever find for puddles
is splashing.    to a large
ditch I almost owed
my death
that the workman saved me

LETTER

his      death
                    finds me
in the news of his death            (there are two prin-
                                    cipal deaths          so far
                                                          though

                            as it's poetry
                you may think more
                            and not be wrong

& as it's poetry
                there are      many
                                loves, many
                truths.
In one

                        two    young men
                                        euphemism
                                        for    boys
                            have fallen
                −climbing
which makes two deaths.   Which is outside the grasp
of this poem and my belief.   We
are elsewhere
                blithe
                    when sobriety
                    knocks
            but

these things do not oppose
                    perhaps
                    are the same
                    you
                    me)

Clambering
Washington
                    1000

                    feet

                    super-
                    conscious

                    & the unconscious
            crustacean                    landing.

                            In the Alps
                            one
                        two
                    three
                four
            five
        almost six                    months
                            mouldering
                            on the talus.

There are gifts there are
connections:

scales there are
musical                    harmonies.   one
                is for Mexico
                one
        is for England
        one
is for potatoes
with sour cream
and CHIVES

                there are
                others.

EVERGLADES PART IV

                              not so easy
                              as it looks
                    as easy as  it looks
as it is easy to look so at ease

it is as easy, so at ease, as it is
                    impossible
  nights of moons
    fan-boat music spanish
      moss and cypress
spiders cover the water we inspect in the easy
                              eternal garden
                    hanging from the trees
snakes napping
& mapping lives  tourists
we are
            temporarily
                              the walls of the boat
                    between us
                              the water
ripples, ripples

            and that SMELL
is easily between us &
the walls of the boat
        paint peeling faster
    as we go faster
and the wind

HELD

you come forward,
held,
& even the moon is/

                where she is

                        calm: comes
                forward:
        climbs stairs:
clears the cats from the chair:

remains.

      "you come forward,
       fully furnished,
       gas fridge &
       steeped in history

             you have counted
             entranced, unattracted
             & you've got them **ALL**
             but

                    who you most wanted
                    antique, heirloom
                    locked in the attic
                    and where's the

     key"

SHARK-FIN SOUP

I.

it was glass. though
                    this is too maybe
                                    old
            a story:
            = the number
        of objects between us
& then)
                    is unbeatable. . .        the story con-
                                        con-
        no, not a committee product, so dis-
                                    tasteful
            to her sensibility/ it was
                            confused
only LAST night NOT
as far
as I thought.

                I was sitting here rapping
                        the bars,
            of my cell, with my spoon,
                                    hungry!
        the guy
brought a SALAD & being hungry!
I began to

though
your friend
    & hers            will get here too
eat: grit: dirt? too        hard THEY WANT TO
                        KILL ME THIS IS A
                        DIAMOND IN BITS IT
                        WILL TEAR MY GUT
                        UP
                  & being
        a cool man
I walked to the door,
                with spoon, to
          the metal latch. I ground a
      while      and it was     GLASS! Some
    body.
   Cheated.
Somebody.


II.

horses, OLD      horses. It was when she
     most wanted
          brilliance of a smile
               running
       wherever he said Get
An Old Horse
& did not mean
       her)    (hearse.

20

There were 7 of us then, counting
my ghost
the witch
& his 4

      selves popping like

              -kernels.

                    NB:
               the Ed. has said
there are those     for whom the above
should be a blank page/ I con-
curred, & suggested

         a mirror

           but the Ed. said
      "at least something empty like
   glass."
So it stayed.

III.

cellini, baby, cellini cellini cellini!

which have few equivalents     sighs,
              bridge of,
          the.     Dunhill,
    a Luxurious Tobacco & the
   Elsenham Brand. His people, good stock,
Anjou, Warwick, a Black Prince or two, some
—where. cheap codas.

                      all the time
                she asks,
something better
than a very      she always says
    good dinner?
                              Yes!


IV.

somewhere under the Atlantic
my message was lost
                    when the sub
                        cut the cable

        all I have left
is ions, ions
            afloat in the ocean.  for you,

                    shark–fin soup?

## STALEMATE

getting up & coming back, getting
            & coming.
                      cigarettes. the
                comb
    of my fingers through
              her hair
           never
  silent, silence

        if he smells it
        he will remember
      sagging ends/
           candles, a
smell of carbon fills the room: beauty even
           in disease
                if not winning
        runs up, or
            away, always

      you think of me
            in motion/ static & too fast
        static
& too fast.
        "is salt (        love)
      from which a sea

can be
made, forever"        sawing
                    gestures near the stomach
                the man is hungry.

    then the CURE: stand
                    straight–kneed, left
                    foot by a pebble: bend
        left              with the          right
                        hand, arm straight &
    lift the pebble/
                return erect/
                            repeat
to replace to earth
her pebble.  this
                remedies sideaches.  for hunger
        food/
                for motion rest/
                                for silence
be silent
        (by repetition we learn reality
        by time repetition
        time by sense
                        & will those
            that would go    further
        please go?      as
    I get fatter
I lose patience.

for the remainder of this poem
I will speak
about chess:
if the ideal game
is not stalemate
we always lose

COLLECT

oboes, bassoon
            the choir tunes
                              tones
                        :resonate walls:
                nitrogen tri-
        iodide on all
THESE PEWS "I really
don't know I never
                really talked to
                                her" detonations
"man them darkies
    BLOCK        really *ran*"
                          service has been
                        reestablished
                effectual, effectual
                                    the words/

 & where he is
            the decision
                        — carved faces
                    is there?

            in her lilac dress
            no bra    breasts        wobble
                                eyeball
                BLOCK

26

                    takes it in
                              for christmas this
                         whip & for
                         you, this saber
     in one ring

                    clarinets, cymbals
               in the middle
                              ruthless violas but
               in the distance
                         on spangled podiums
                                        three  sliding
                         rules jangle
I hear it
but I cannot see it
so I disbelieve
               though that nitrogen
                                   is REAL
*BLOCK*

                    why then refer to me?
               "It was not
          the caress of her lips"
                                   father at his
                              golf
                    & who is at
                    the cow, painting
                                        *BLOCK*

               when it explodes:
     charred select
filter paper

"a flight of birds

               streaks

                          into  the distance"

 & rules
jangle

takes the liana to hand and he IS coming watch
your
        sipapu!        dance!       throw sand!
                          *BLOCK*
                 "the length of him"
              all these
                highjackers some must be
                  FBI/CIA/YOU

      said it
    properly. in dialect
to the marching elders

thumb pages & this:

           is how we celebrate
         the atom
          for this is the
                TWENTIETH
          century

please the fleas
                for they need your
        blood "that he was
                    looking for," sent.

    If it is only a matter of preference we are all
*BLOCK*
        lost (again oboes, bassoon. . .)

where pines take over
from the aspen
one is closer to poles or god
                        though your tongue
                    will be constant
                ("but the back of her throat")

    **YOUR MONEY!**

TITLED

> this ashtray is an old can
> w/o a label this ashtray
> stolen from a NYC hotel
> this from the College Spa
> this purchased at a five
> & dime and this the   prize
> walked out of a cafeteria
> **KOEBENHAVNS UNIVERSITET**

a pastry plate, while
cigarettes cost $1.25/pack

And this is where the world
this is where she
is

> catcalls. "weak tread
> on the back stairs
> half a century
> settling
> has brought this
> skew, this
> rot
> though wood had
> the full measure"

& these animals passing

hold   their own
      to            arc
                    breathless at the end


the lack of foundation
typical for those times
               AND earthquakes
            remodellings
        plus the inheritance
        plus the tax
                    no one
                is too poor
                to pay but
      who can carry the purchase away,
                single-handed?

all I have to go on
            is
      his testimony

          & you know what that is:
                     for
                we are all
                kleptomaniacs
            of the mind

(Mirrors in your room,
he said, leaning
and hanging.)

## CALLIOPE

\*

in your spare equation
the notes men make
on your shrilling
pipes
are less than
& the same to you. in your
most spare equation
you are the world
you are willing
to be happy.

your affair goes on, over coffee
"I can get pregnant easily
tho I can't bear"
perhaps he has a plain wife
& takes up graffiti
but I can't face
the stained glass in your bedroom
I can't face your perpetual citation of nietzsche
whatever calliope I may have said
I cannot face.

fitful, fidgety
my friends stretch far

inhabiting the world
new lands for them & no news comes/
but new friends.  you
appear to be different:
it is for you
your world lives &
you are pleased;
I think you are alone.

*

clearly I am relenting.  for afterwards
there was a carnival
in his eyes, children
on his fingers.  he thought he was
a roller-coaster
holding his belt with one hand
waving his hat with the other.
his eyes were wild
& he came up to me saying
Brother?
it was a nice day
& he drew closer around him
cotton candy & boys
& girls & took
what he wanted, most.

even the bird in your backyard
thought he was a carnival
& played medleys
on the power line.

hot dog, soda:
I walked away from the concession
to forget all his words
I overheard, underfed

\*

but then you can't bear
the hall of mirrors
while he is mostly
invisible,
making you
& I can't face
that time, the look on your face
when he led you
to the hall of horrors
"Jim always wants me to be
perfect you know. I
warned him. I said
Jim I'll be perfect
then I won't need you

any more"
& then the lonely
the electric
calliope

*

maybe he thinks of a maze?      then
I'll do more justice:
it is not
a collection of right
& left turns.
we seldom get as close
as contact
but it is not a maze/

muse/ I get
desperate:
out almost of control &
past patience:
while my friends fear
secretaries.
I have almost decided to leave
but I always see the horizon
the horison is flat
& far

AND near, softer than
the well-worn flesh of your body
 & softer than that
 & in general softer than the silence here
when the carnival
is over.

\*

it is
sitting on a runway
close to skidmarks, midnight
there is no matter of life & death
in which we're helpless.
you disagree, but
we are only helpless in a matter of death.

I am waiting
to see your face
when you leave
the hall of horrors —
you will laugh
you will take an airplane/
when you land
I'll be there, trying to avoid
telling you something

& that
is poetry.

don't blame me
when I fuck
in monosyllabics,
or if I want you more for preferring him to me.

\*

your language calliope & my concession
the south wind
full of dust
as the rain comes/
is calliope in a carnival & your eyes
clear)
we are all settlers
in the rain:
the park is not ours
& mostly we seek
shelters/
I have sent barking after you
my lonely concession my
calliope my only concession.

at least he won't come here
it is too clean
& smells
like ammonia.  yes you
& also like dogfood
are welcome to join me
tho I will establish conditions:
that you like trees &
think of me
as I think of you
otherwise I might continue
talking about love
in your absence & not
in your presence.

\*

"at the gates," shrill, shrill
you are about to go home
he is alone on the model train
circling the park
tho it seems like spring
the squirrel goes on crying
These expeditions of solipsists!

of course he never threatened you:
he promised only those miracles
he could perform.
I would do better but
as I heave my last ball
at the bottles
I hardly care that
not one of them
hit you.    you *would* "think, on so small an island,
all Irishmen must be alike;
but it is not so."

*

there is a fineness
in their bodies —
discriminations
more significant
than their minds/
I will not repeat what he said
but his stance when he told you
was a far stretch
in mumbletypeg.

come then; your

tryst, your
yellow jeep:
"I felt/ not obligated
to entertain him but
I had to say something."

there are strictures,
the engines are turning off;
the latest canopy I pass
is pretty.  the thing
has so many pipes &
pictures, so much
paint,  so much
gilt & so
happy

goodbye
calliope

## YOUR SKIN AFTER THE FUCK YOUR SMELL ON MY HANDS

Bangle
the year goes
(december) im-
  mersion
            a rattling,
      liquid nitrogen
is not like
a woman
's treachery

      the year going
      — december —

                  a minute
                  of nitrogen
                  & any hand dies

this whole hour
& what
        for a poem
                              & what
for misgivings,
        your indian's giving

— our bangle for december

## MUSIC FOR FERGUSON

like wind chimes a block away
panes bumping
& the plastic alarm clock
also expanding & contracting
clicks
my frame creaks
through the cheap sofa
like hunting shells on the shore
— surely enough
to choose from

# ENDING THE NOVEL

for David Warren

a matter of finding
zero
& increasing
the frequency

     collusion of extras

         , a left
        -ward
     movement
   if you face a
map:

potatoes    |       iced.
yr bread    |
lamb       |   hanging
        "where it balanced"
  noiseless

you are as full
as a new sack of sugar

"look"

    air on both
    sides of the window
  mouths on both sides
    which call this poem
      Music for Ferguson 2

a pear tree outside
the window
sickle pears

what cartography is
to a mapmaker

is a beginning
— some people can
isolate emotions
like isotopes — but
an amateur

rocks, rain, wind
scales on a viola
"wanting to be all men"
(like a jukebox

## BODY

not untouched. this
  essay
  this peering
trial

apologies, & I begin
like the girl in the window,
dressing

 & a machine to measure
porosity

one or two rocks, three
from a history of rocks .
a hone

keep your anger
/ for tomorrow
keep your change
/for the ferry

not all fools
are immune/

or not good enough
poorly prepared
for an age of evil,
poorly paid

ready to break down

but which eyes
in this city
follow,

how does this window focus?

## WALKING & EATING POEM

**I.**

stratum, -a
                delineations
            of stone
    what the palm
        remembers

how eyes go
camellia, 1970, southern
        california, ditto, check.

            the palm has lines
            to fit the stone
            to
die is a line

**II.**

partly flowers
in your hair

partly flowers
in your mouth

    *an indian trick
    for diminishing
    thirst

simile as the savor
  of saliva,
    mouth's pebble,
      stone's mouth

## III.

or grapejuice
         (counting 12, 13)
  lemonade.   & one
     sleeping,
       for whom this line
beacons.

("am I overamping on res-
pectability?")

     . whose line
    . beckons

19)
  whose hands found fault
       -lines,

    walking

## SEVENTY-FIFTH MAGNILOQUENT

the neighbors' merriment
  squeezing from the tube
    "talk a strange"

waitresses in the john's prediction of
                predilection for numbers
                          whose phrase

ends at the end of the line ] [
                    knocked, , , knocked up.

      as befits the landscape
      scoring low, scoring well

   the squeegee OR id is more
  benign
than the ego
          or eyes  .  this portrait
           has windows have

     cleansed or not
transparency.

screwing in plasma
fucked in the kitchen
   where nectarines

           ripen
          were it a nasty poem
        frozen waitresses would
        in the coldness of motion
        watch the fruit rot / serve mould.

   we are freed by the  number we salvage.
                    Always
              it is the logic of abortion
         fails, the fear
        of an expanded joke,
      shrinking cock

The landscape I soar to
  squeezed from laughing
    scores phrases in the  wall
     remnants of
       etched in the mirror
         blinds me

## SCRIVENER

as you applied the salve
there were stories,

            how your sun

        burnt:

    flowers

          coolly pointed back to your eyes:

  I am learning a limit to this business.   a bloodletter's

w/ fear,

        should whichever star we know
     ferry, what soul

            foundering to peace,
ANOTHER rescue on the delta of time,

               or fling?
       you could fail to forgive my enquiry.

a patrician's           trade/

             squishing the words of this world

          a wall higher from your glance;
    an "omen of wail"

savior & catch-all of the world. a shell at your shore,
believe me, a gringo's gone but listens,

             trans

## IN CONCERT

1.

top of the hill, oaks.   a wind
moving the oaks.

   in your mind I saw karyatids forming.

the rest of the  week/ no talking/
            just hummed like pipes,
            fixed the truck.

2.

      there were more of us
in more places
than I could handle.   & then fewer.

   I saw five people step into a redwood
            & saw the redwood
                  vanish.

this was in technicolor. & yes,
I believe in elves.

      they are marvelous creatures,
      better than us
      & planning their improvement.


3.

water came down the cliff
gray diorite darkened
& sparkled.

      we leaned & twisted
   to catch one stream
     full-face,
   & swallow. The question posed,
     of inheritance,
      who is good enough?

## POEM ABOUT CONTROL & THE CRADLE
## OF CIVILIZATION

a question about reality     .     its embossure on the mind

the interaction we call control

.

the units of control
are plans
whose measure/
cradling time/
is time.

for months I plan
to go to the shoe store
& buy boots

w/ these boots
I will walk,

long hikes,
learn the plants

& souvenir
the birdcalls.

For months I plan these walks,
  the boots,
      the boots' poems.
                   I decide to begin
               w/ buying boots
           reflections on a shoe store,
            smells, chairs,
        the shoehorn the clerk
       handles so much it is like
    a longer and thinner hand.

I have had the boots for two weeks,
       no walks taken,
I will detain you long enough
  to claim that
when dealing w/ reality,
    mostly I flail,
           how gears work
        in transmissions, chance
         in cards, or choosing
       from the muted colors
           of my socks.

              Also there is your hot
          smile, your matter-of-fact
         way of pulling your panties off;

    & when you have me slavering
I am speechless & flail.

1/24/71


I am visiting Boston, you L.A.
It is our first anniversary. I will call
you, billing our number in Trumansburg.
It is snowing but we will still talk
instantaneously through the miles
of weather, across rivers and plains,
up and back the same mountains and over
the land of bison, crossing the paths of
gradual imperceptible migrations —
tribes for whom our *totem* meant
*sister's vulva* — we will talk across
the time of mastodons, dinosaurs,
over churning waves of the Great
Inland Sea, glowing lava on the
shrinking crust of a planet
— our spontaneous voices
dangling in the universe —
singing the range of love

# EXCERPTS FROM THE CARTESIAN NOTEBOOK

"the part of the body in which the soul
exercises its functions immediately
is in nowise the heart, nor the whole
of the brain, but merely the most inward
of its parts, to wit, a certain very small
gland which is situated in the middle
of its substance."

— Rene Descartes

"Basically the pineal gland
is light sensitive; the substance
secreted by this gland is mimicked
by LSD."

— T F. J. Martin

\* \*

my stove, Sterling 403          sitting

a four-foot distance

& the hour is

later:

this   is the dramatic ((

black cat eyes four
oh three

let x be me

x  is

be coming the cat,

fever in the eyes flicking
tail & tongue . singed

fur as the wood swells to spark
y      the "culmination of the
known into the unknown" the "primal
hoard of recognition for all
that lacks time"

at low values of x
y nears the skin . .

spot yr ball
& let me putt :

there are 5 equally
good ways to
love a woman & the same for
a man: already you do
not believe me! but I am in the hole


))
moment:

in the kitchen sit & smoking
late w/ less to
overhear

focused on the cat focused
on the fire in the stove

(403)

to see with the cat's eyes to consist
in the pendulum twitch of that
four-footed tail is not enough.


but blasted with the wood!     IS

this is the first way   .   the last is this
poem which insists on the first

in between we say
"I love you"

\* \*

*he speaks*

say, this     wax.   It has just been
extracted from the

                honey/comb; it has not completely
              lost the taste of the honey; it
                  retains

          some of the smell of the flowers
            from which it was gathered; its
colour,
shape, size are manifest;

it is hard     ,     cold, and easily handled, &

GIVES OUT A SOUND if you rap it with your
                              knuckle. . . .

the wax is put by the fire!  It loses

the remains of its flavour, the fragrance
evaporates, the colour

changes, the shape is LOST,

the size *increases*, it
becomes fluid & hot, it can

.

hardly be
handled,

AND IT WILL NO LONGER GIVE OUT A SOUND IF
YOU RAP IT

* *

& signed off, plussed.

no use
particularizing
my experience

(more than it was)

dozens danced
moaning
in Urdu

I didn't catch it all
     — something about sunshine, pome

          granates —

wearing togas, muttering Greek
we were weaving through
⟦thronged masses⟧

      hawkers selling rings, tins of
      cinnamon, slaves for purposes
    a Michelin to Provence

It seems crazy & out of place
  in a poem about epistemology
          but

        what if I told
        my real dream?
    I was building a table
  working hard, in the woods
      a stranger, quiet
     & dark, walked
      towards me: I kept
    working
        four feet off
    he stopped & I looked

         at his black shirt, his
      black head & black mask
 & his terrible smile

then I was writing a poem
at the table; someone came in
& walked around the house
but I didn't get up  .  later
he came thru the doorway:
tall, strong, cast a big shadow.
When he sat down I looked at him, his
shirt & mask & his grin

\* \*

*his malignant demon speaks*

yr extremities
I sever first.
       I keep
yr luscious trunk
& all its cavities
for my pleasure, alive
& cauterized  .  I feed you

yr sister's tits.
           I stress
the reality of the senses,
announce the rule of time

           then I throw you in the fire so it's not so noisy.


\* \*


it's not like there was a
*program*
           coordinating my actions
               w/ yours around
                      (how many)
                  cookfires   ,   turning
              from wash-dishes-in-smoke
              to unroll-bags-in-tent,

                at dusk   .   all friends
                silent & present

             we enlarge to a campfire
      as the NIGHT

Is there some series of tasks some constant
ritual,
      subsistence farming
            berry gathering
                    building
    each night's fire
           in a different
                clearing

would be enough? we ask
& tell jokes . as the cold
           worsens we get
           melancholy

           crawl into tents:

           all night my toes
           rub zippered corners

\*\*

old corn
stalks
bannered
antennae on
cars moving

times as under
great winds it all
looks like graphs

motion per
pendicular
direction,
leaves right
angle stalks

   *as a plumbline*'s
   *impartial will*
    *I judge*

so many people
think of
   virtue
as a "pure
white pleasantly
scented cream
of cosmetic
consistency.
Greaseless, non-
staining, non-
irritating. In-
stantly lethal
to male sperm."

\*\*

| denied | consider | Watchman, what |
|--------|----------|----------------|
| glass (ground) | sensation | as sex |

"permits total absorption into non-being"

| distinguished | consider me | useless |
|---------------|-------------|---------|
| to survive | mental | near |
| power | late | sighted |
|  | only | blind |
|  |  | distinctions |

what are leaves? asked Teddy
they gave him glasses, he
became president, glasses
are no damn good

tri
angulation : : lamb , veal
     & lamentation .

                    who puts
     it to her has no claim       just
            as there is no punctuation
          to mark sorrow
      is there no claim to justice.

reduced to angles & distances , distinct calculus,
landscape without
               a curve's shelter, just

     the surreal, sour arc of food
          from plate to mouth,

nine months in the womb
& a fuzzy spot of dying.

PRESERVING THE CHURCH
                    *for* Alan Pike
                        FREEING PIGEONS
POEM WITH FOUR TITLES


focus now
on our feet
   surprised by the noises
         our feet & breathing

                    rustles &

            clutter:
            long aisle, to the side


   — we are selved,
-conscious. I listen
      to our feet, listening

                    the long nave
            four in the morning
         old church, it is dawning

                    *consider* waking
the length of this side aisle
long nave, all that
            we make / passing
         with our time & bulk this
      space & time in the morning

   a
cross (the apse

              hurried from
                        larger
           echoes /
                       aisle
circling the choir         our scaffold is
                        where we left it.  we
                mix a batch
                of plaster.

          "suppose we used another
            door, wore ear
              plugs, still
         got here from there
               —what changes"
                              with trowels slap
                        plaster onto boards
              climb scaffolding pipes &
                  planks.
the pipes squeek to
    our weight, wood
  sounds we jostle
      trowels
              & boards
                        & banging
       pant more as we climb.

                   we are so
                   high! half

as high
the dim light slides
from windows
to floor, no longer
think
of our feet /
our trowels turn
& flash        pressing
plaster        into cracks. this
is why they pay
us to repair
if this is repair
stationed
on planks in the air no
knowledge of the
weather filling
cracks with plaster
"about time, why
should we get paid? lost
as we are to it,
wholly gone,
wholly here, or
if we could be paid?"  "you
freed the pigeons janitors
tried to trap"

splashing plaster covers
clothes & trowels, into hair, WE

"disappear in the work" in the air
trowels sound
on the wall. it
        is evening.

                we ache.

                                we
        climb down & down to
    noise of shoes
                in apse & length of nave
                                at dawn
                on that day we
                        climb

            to a rose
        window sing drinking
            songs for the mass, tango
        on our planks & plant
explosives "this
is the application
            of knowledge
        every
    destruction IS
    creation
what is said"
                    we suspend
                    in the dome
        as the dome crumbles & float
                        away from wreckage, who
                will find our bodies

          to blame or pay? do we
          misuse our minds, marking time
on our bones? on
  our own bones
                    chanting in
                  paradise. we nearly, we
                never finish
                      tomorrow

going to work in the church
   there is this
          souvenir, this
                    tangible & plaster slab

          in the shape of words:

*I am lonely. I look*
*for things / to repair,*
*to lose*
*all the pay of pride*

and take this—
                  in some place of our soul
                —this patch
                      & flapping, call

          KNOTS & SPLICES, no end
                of screaming

$2.95

David McAleavey (b. Wichita, Kansas, 1946) has been involved in recent years in both East and West Coast poetry. He has an A.B. from Cornell University (1968), and spent a year doing graduate work at U. C. Berkeley. At present he is pursuing the M.F.A. and Ph.D. at Cornell.

"The situations that David McAleavey describes are not unusual ones. And yet these poems hold our attention, they hint at greater depths and more resonant meanings than our first reading of them may allow. I think the secret here (as in good poetry and fiction everywhere) lies in the combinations, in an intuited connection among the parts which, when we catch it, illuminates the whole. Perhaps this is just a fancy way of saying that McAleavey in this first book of poems gives a sense of new possibilities to the familiar world. As a reader of poems and an inhabitant of that world, I'm grateful."

James McConkey

*Other books in the Ithaca House poetry series:*

Stuart Peterfreund  *The Hanged Knife & Other Poems.* Stephen Shrader  *Leaving by the Closet Door.*  Robert Allen  *Valhalla at the OK.*  Frederick Buell  *Theseus & Other Poems.*  Robert Patton  *Thirty-Seven Poems: One Night Stanzas.*  Karen Hanson  *Spine.*  Greg Kuzma *Song for Someone Going Away.*  Joseph Bruchac  *Indian Mountain.*  Peter Wild  *Peligros.*  All $2.95.  Ronald Silliman  *Crow.*  $1.95.  Raymond DiPalma  *The Gallery Goers.*  $1.50.  *Forthcoming:*  Ralph Salisbury  *The Ghost Grapefruit & Other Poems.* William Hathaway  *True Confessions & False Romances.* Danny Rendleman  *Trees Moving and We Can't Hear Them.*  John Moore  *By Selkirk's Lake & Other Poems* All $2.95.  David Melnick  *Eclogs.*  $1.95.